A Treasury of Plants

For
Anne-Marie

To John and Margaret — happy Christmas and a healthy 2021, All good wishes, David. Dec. 2020

A Treasury of Plants

David Donaldson

Wynstones Press

Published by

Wynstones Press

Stourbridge
England.

www.wynstonespress.com

First edition 2020

Cover photographs courtesy of Neil Moore
© moore-photographics.com

Printed in UK.

ISBN 9780 946206 889

*"We should live life
on earth the way plants do.
They remain fixed to the earth
but they transform it
and evolve it."*

Omraam Mikhael Aivanhov

Contents

Tree of Life

Seed Knowledge

Celebrations

Afterwords

And Finally

Glossary

By the Same author

Acknowledgement:
I would like to acknowledge my indebtedness to the work of botanist
Gerbert Grohmann (1897-1957)

Stunned

by the sky's
sublime serenity,

the garden's returning life
out of the blue;

how it's come about,
this dome of air that's

warmth and light and life
thrusting back

the warring opposition
of black and white.

Easter Sunday 2019

Around the Year

Snowdrop

Galanthus. 'Milk flower'.

Stationary clusters on the move
Throughout January. Long blades
Curving on the air from bulb-
Barracks underground; gesturing
To right and left as if granting
Clearance to green spathes
Rising spear-like on slender stems
And sealed to secure the treasure,
Flat-packed. Even so, slits
In the papery membrane
Give hints and glints of white.

Along verges, in back gardens,
Churchyards, stately garden walks,
They muster, clustering
To attention as stems reach
Full height, release tear-drops
To hang by a single thread,
White pearl caskets sealed
Three-fold, two layers deep
And opening to form a bell
Whose note is what our seeing
Hears: a fruiting body ringing in
The season's change, attracting
To itself the busy interest of ants.

Bold, snow-white pioneers, among
The first to risk their heads above
Earth's parapet, launch the offensive
To re-colonise wasted ground.

We call them *White Ladies,*

The Fair Maids of February.

Daffodil Rescue

A late attack. Temperatures tumbling
Through a starry night, the brittle grass
Crunching to the tread, sheathed spears
Of daffodils too tall, too soon advanced

Lose their sun-alignment, are skewed
In all directions overnight. We snap
The rigid stems, bring them into warmth.
Vases of water reinstate them upright,

Green rockets capped with a tapered
Capsule, a packed mission to deliver.
Time passes. The warmth indoors
Ignites a slow measured countdown.

One by one they swell to their tips
Until the papery seals give way and there-
Wide streaks of earth-bound yellow
Packed and ready to rise to their appointed

Tasks. Overnight, unseen in the lingering
Warmth of the living room, the corolla
Unwraps, pale petals first, outer, then inner,
Two folded sets of three extending wide

To release their transformed pedicel:
Green stalk become golden, all crown,
Fanfare, speech from the throne; no
Show of gilded hollow power but

An open invitation to approach
And see: enter the royal pavilion,
Carry off the gold dust. And all for free!

Crocus

Showy garden riches.

The narrow tubes, fuel-fed
From underground, are packaged
Floral fireworks, enclosed in pale
Waxy casings, and delivered
On the chill air for the sun
To strike its match. Out spurt
Puffs of flame: there's Lilac Prayer
And Purple Death, Virgin White
And Golden Resurrection; closed
Caskets, unclasping to serve:
Drink up the offered sun, sample
The new year's vintage, affirm
The feasting has begun. And,
Having done, it's very soon they
All keel over, flat on their sides,
Like so many shrunk balloons.

Be my Valentine?

14 February 269 AD

So you're born blind and hoping
One day you'll see? Valentine's
A Christian priest and healer who
Agrees to treat you, instruct you
In the faith, teach you to pray,

Whose healing works its cure
As light begins to dawn for you,
(And night to overshadow him,
Sentenced for marrying couples
Contrary to Imperial decree).

The night before he's clubbed
To death and has his head cut off,
He hands a note to be passed
To you, the World's first Valentine.
No pierced hearts, red roses,

Question marks. 'From your
Valentine' it reads, enclosing
A victory token marking
His last hours: a golden-yellow
  Crocus flower.

The Wild Bunch

Wild daffodils

In the prairie of the meadow.
Pioneers arrived mysteriously
A few years ago and spreading
Year on year: a few blooms
Multiplied to a score in four years;

Blind spathes staking out future
Territory while their fruitful elders
Consolidate the home patch
Facing every direction except
Due north and less showy than

Lanky domesticated types liable
To bend, flop or fall flat under
A blustery shower. They grow
Closer to home, retain balance,
Well-adjusted, nodding on the breeze,

As yet a modest star-cluster:
The Pleiades rather than the never-
Ending Milky Way. Yet, precious
Enough for us to shut the gate
On the sheep, leave them

Holding sway.

Primrose

No bulb-cradle nor starry stem
Springing out of its cot, but a rosette
Of veined and netted leaves pouring
Out of a flowering heart. First rose

Of Spring, Easter rose, so named
And not even one of the family!
Shallow-rooted, still bunched close
To earth and bearing neither stem

Nor thorns. Salver blossoms
On such thin threads of stalks;
All wide open innocence, all
Tender hope on the awakening air,

Facing into life its dreamy blossoms,
Thrum and pin, thrum and pin.
Beetle, bumblebee enter in,
Pin and thrum, pin and thrum,

Beetle, bumblebee, will they come?

Ash Wednesday

This is the day for wearing ash
And a long face. And it's just
As the new year's set to spring
To life. Beneath our feet they lie:

The seeds and bulbs given over
To the earth. Unquestioning,
Still; silent in the dark. Attending
On the Call. And in due course

It comes: sun-kiss, rainbow-shower.
Then off come the coverings of ash.
The solemn sleep is over, the bridegroom
Is at hand. Bit by bit and in good time

They ready themselves. Out of a slit
Of green: the light, the dawn, the ever-
New fragrance of the bridesmaids
That attend the circling year.

Wood Anemone

Threads passed through the golden eye of the sun,
And the woods embroided with fresh-faced flowers,
Each a white star nodding above frills of green
And feathering the woodland: a carpet of honour

Unrolled from underground and extending year
On year, to ray in all directions ankle-deep
About the stationary trees. *Windflowers*, swaying
In greeting as the god blows in. Or are they

A dewfall of tears? Balm for Aphrodite's grief,
For Adonis lost? *Flowers of Death*, according
To the Chinese. Soon to disappear as if they'd
Never been- or nothing more than threads.

Marsh Marigold

Caltha palustris

Goblets brimming with early Spring's
Intoxicating sun-liquor, impacting
On the wetlands, the dull marsh:

Largesse of shiny heart-shaped leaves,
Bud-buttons cupped together in nurseries,
Become golden goggle-eyes, sprung

Out of their leaf-cots and swelling
Fit to burst with sunshine. Old
Water Boots, ancient survivor

Of marshlands long since drained;
The *Mayflower* favoured to put wind
Into the sails of the Pilgrim Fathers;

Otherwise known as *Meadowbright*,
Crazy Beth, *Water Goggles*, *May Blob*..
Or *Marsh Marigold* to sanctify the Waste?

And still spreading its brief riot of golden
Brilliance beside secluded woodland lakes,
Where to tread is to trespass on unruffled

Reflections, settled silences.

The Lesser Celandine

A favourite of Wordsworth's, a noxious
Weed to some. And not one to hide away
When Winter's done, but first out of the blocks.

Club-like tubers, floral stick-grenades launch
An explosive Spring advance; a cheerful riot
Of glossy rounded leaves, each the launch pad

For a stalk topped by a knob of green that's
Glowing inside and finely tuned to the new
Year's growth of Sun. So one fine day, you find

The bare rocky margins of the pond a swamp
Of *Brighteyes*: glossy yellow organ stops pulled out
To the full: Sun's swelling fanfare on *the joys to come*,

And signal, too, that soon you'll have to set
To work on the tubercles forming in the axils
Of the leaves to keep in measure bounds

The spreading joys of the Lesser Celandine.

Bluebell

The Nation's favourite.
Long-settled status to half
The World's population;
Acres of nodding *Bell-Bottles*
Criss-crossing the woods
On cue before the leafing trees
Have veiled the Sun.

They're youthful signs of age
And continuity; ethereal haze
Of violet-blue; summons
To dream or wakefulness?
Lady's Nightcap yet dedicated
To St George, the root sap
Once glueing feathers to arrows.

Bluebell: still hitting the mark;
Stealing the show from
Snowdrop, Crocus, Daffodil,
Lighting up the woodlands
With a fragrant, prayerful glow.
When they retreat to leaves
Spring is through and Summer

Holds the floor. Leaf by leaf
Their carpet unravels. What's
Left sleeps on dreamless, lost
To view till Sun and Earth
Reconfigure the measured dance
Prompting their magic cue.

Stitchwort

Stelleria holostea

Wedding guests in matching white
Bunched together on the bank, wide
Faces upturned for the Sun's photograph;

Concealed beneath the cheerful smiles,
Are they holding one another up? Those
Elongated stems, thin as sparrow legs

And elbow-angled sharply at the joints:
Dead man's bones liable to snap? A remedy
For broken limbs? Then the leaves,

Wide-stepped in opposing pairs, abrupt
And straight as arrow heads, nodal points
From which flower-bearing stems

Shoot out either side of the leading stem:
Remedy for the stitch? A *Thunder Flower*
If picked? Never mind the old tales.

Wedding guests in matching white
Clustered star-like on the bank,
Whose wedding are you celebrating

Colour-captured by the light?

Columbine

First, lobed leaves in whorls swept
Out of the earth, unfurling in threes
Upon threes of branching stalks,

The leading shoots mounting
Above the rising dome of green
And rigid with the leap

From leaf to bud; multiple threes
Transform to perfect fives,
Pentagonal bells suspended from

The slenderest of pinnacles;
Or *five birds together*, wings blue
As Mary's mantle sheltering
The hollow nectaries within,
Whose inmost stores

Are like drops held in their beaks.
Columbine: pure faith, hope,
Longing. For what is all that beauty
Without the loving attention
Of her soul-partner, the bee?

Spring Rain

The garden's smoking in mist
And brimming after rain.
Reach to cut a lilac branch

And a shower's shaken
To shiver you awake.
The filled pond's motionless,

Mirror-clear, the birds
Their own full stream of song.
The clouds have spoken,

Grey on grey for a night
And a day. The cracked
Earth's resealed and dark

As rich mould. Columbines,
Toppled by the downpour,
Lie stretched out on the lawn,

And Cow Parsley, its pride
Of umbels lifted to the sky
Is now bowed so low

They brush the ground
Bent in recognition
Of what has just passed by.

Cow Parsley

Familiarity breeds contempt.
A rampant weed fit only for cows?

And thanks to near-relations
Hemlock, Fool's Parsley,

It's branded *Devil's Meat, Mother die,*
Raising the alarm that to sample it

Might do you harm.

*

Feathery foliage, a rabbit delicacy,
Long stems once prized peashooters;
Its strength lies in spreading underground

So come the Spring it's ever-ready,
Rising along the verges in unbroken
Waves of white. Spring's snow-blossom

Giddy with fragrance

Waving the world back to life;
Massed umbels of confetti;
Lady's lace in the height of fashion;

A Whitsun assembly, crowding
The margins of the meadows;
Wild celebrants in the presence

Of the flowering grasses.

The Grasses

Rock-a-bye-baby on the tree top

Shafts of sunlight taken root.
The sward of Eden transferred
To Earth for a soft landing;

Endlessly provident whether cut,
Crushed, trampled, browsed or grazed.
Selfless as water or air, irrepressible

Returning life. Where are its full-
Rounded leaves, its gorgeous blossoms?
Slimmed to the thinest of jointed stems,

Curled sheaths sharpened with finest silica,
Blossoms no more than spikes, ears,
Or feathery panicles drying to gold

On the summer breeze and rippling
Like dry waves over acres. Warmth,
Light: Sun's still-living language.

For *down will come cradle, baby and all*
Onto the green and golden Earth,
  The Grasses at our service.

White Lilac

Snowfall out of the blue.
But nothing to shiver about:
Each curled four-lobed blossom
A tongue of fire,

The clustered panicles
Alight with the broadcast
Fullness of their fragrance;

At least that's what your nose
Relays, reaching to inhale
What they have to say:

A wake-up glimpse
Into how the World might be:

Snowfall out of the blue
Become the Dove
Descended into the Lilac tree.

Lily

The first sweet breath of morning
And the lily to attention on its slender stem,
Mirrored in the hush of the pond's
Seamless surface; twin top-heavy
Trumpet-blossoms raised on the air,
Virgin-white and incandescent.
Green streaks delving into deep-
Gorged throats of whiteness,
Curled edges peeled back in six
To broadcast the distillation
Of all that spiralling growth.

Exchange gifts! Your amazed
Attention for these – summer's
White-woven wedding pavilions,
Seeded shooting stars of soothing fragrance:

Annunciation of heart's ease.

Rose

Petals, scent draw us in,
Enfold us no less
Than the visiting bees.
Earth attained
To its flowering summit,

The Sun drawn down
In fullest measure
To reconfigure Paradise –
And not content, bursting
Into fruit on the family tree:

Apple, Pear, Cherry, Plum,
Blackberry, Strawberry...
The fruiting Pentagram
And Rose its crowning blossom,
The woody network of roots

Drawing from earth-darkness
The sustenance required.
Rose is the Kingdom come;
On Earth as in Heaven;

Mary cradling her Child
In a rose-bower; Dante
In rose-petalled paradise;
It's the one World inwoven:
On a stem of thorns.

Wild Strawberry

Shallow-rooted, invasive.
The basal rosette's a fountain
Of unfurling leaves, three
To each slender furry stem.
Runners strike out in all

Directions, grow to stretch
A sunny canopy, a low-spreading
Festival marquee of green.
So Strawberry settles in, self-
Invited, swarms over

The rockery, dominates
The margins of the pond,
Star-standards announcing
Five white petals about a heart
Of gold: the tribe of Rose.

And yet such shallow roots?
All summer-long their sun-
Bright blossoms blush into
Small sweet fruits dipping
Into their own green shade.

Crouching, close to Mother,
Lacking any stem to stand,
Strawberries can only sprawl:
The crawling, creeping baby
Of the family. *Strew*berry's

The true genesis of the name.
But as for sweet inoffensiveness,
What sharp temptations lurk!
Spotted with strawberries
The mislaid handkerchief

That set Othello on the rack.
And Virgil warned of innocent
Appearences. For our snake
In the grass translate: *the snake*
Among the strawberry leaves.

Poppy

mixed species and papaver
somniferum in particular

Surface attachment. No firm grip
On earth. Milky sap an analgesic
And addictive drug. Buds hang
Drooping as if weighed in thought.

Crushed inside, the short-lived
Scarlet petals are paper party dresses
Wrinkled free by the Sun. Soon,
They disconnect, one by one, hang

Wide like wings ready for flight.
We wear them to remember.
Blood shed. Lives sacrificed. Oh
The irony of our choice! Poppy,

Swaying us to sleep and dream-
Illusions, petals falling spent to earth
Leaving deaths-heads rattling
In their wake, dried out on a stalk.

Seeds spring up in multitudes,
Frail-rooted beauty partying
Once more; they yield us
Temporary pain relief; dreams

Of escape in which to waste away;
But as for banishing war, peace
Our surface-attachment
Poppy-frail. Or how deep set?

Proof against fear and the addictive
Delusions of power
                           riches
                                   glory?

Sunflower

The Summer tiptoe on its pole,
Its one expansive eye wide
Open, tracking the passage
Of the sun. It's dressed

For the occasion: flaring frills
Of yellow petals, face bronzed dark
As the furry bees which settle
To sip the goodness it receives.

And then – it's done: it's drunk
Its fill of sun. Its flare of petals
Dies away: they curl and shrink,
The shorn head begins to droop,

The deep gaze glazes over,
Inclines earthwards by degrees.
All that upright sunward glory
Hunches over. It looks so sad,

The huge head hung in seeming sorrow.
It makes you want to weep, indulge
In melancholy, forget all
About its fruit of teeming seeds.

Tree of Life

Earth's Alive,

A Tree of Life inseparable
From its field of stars,
Mankind its crowning fruit

Or burning crown? Its blood
Is water, liquid currency
Exchanged for endless growth

And put to use in all extremities
Of light and dark, of heat and cold.

At the Poles

The stars neither rise nor set.
They might as well be bolted
To the sky for water's locked

In ice and earth imprisoned
In permafrost through the long
Polar night. Life's driven

To shelter in the root. Stem
And leaf contract and harden
As if welded to the ground.

The world's divided into
Black and white; some weeks
Of daylight, months of night,

Above, Earth's fertile field
Of stars. As the Spring sun
Hangs low on the horizon

And the ground frost thaws,
Flowers blaze briefly out of
Crevices and stunted

Cushion-mounds reflecting back
In form and colour, star-light,
Sunlight; and all the crystal purity

Of the polar sky.

At the Equator

All night, the horizon lies open to the stars;
By day the Sun's sheer climb reaches the zenith,
Swallowing your shadow at noon. The earth's
Drenched with shafts of light. Rain clouds

Muster in the humid air, as thunder growls
And lightning ignites a brief intensity of rain.
Here, Earth grows to its full measure; trees
Reach gigantic heights, festooned pillars,

Each a garden where lianas drape their tapestries,
Embroided with blue grape clusters or flowers
Of fiery sparks with colourful birds and butterflies;
While ferns and orchids as if tossed aloft, pour

Out of crevices and hollows high in the trees.
The eye's drawn up and up but cannot penetrate
To the sky. Sunlight filters through the forest crown
Of rambling canopies and what's reflected back

From the dim-lit forest floor are all the colours
Of the rainbow; leaves, flowers, fruits impossible
To disentangle as if all the twining stems were one
Within the forest's all-embracing Earth cathedral.

In the Desert

The green pasture of the Promised Land,
The spreading shade of the soft leaf,
Has shrivelled to baked earth beneath
An unsparing sky. It's reduced

To flattened forms, squat globes,
Monumental pillars: waxed stems
Of fleshy fibre tough as leather,
Some fortified with spikes like

Hardened solar rays. Here's home
In water's absence within a ring
Of fire. Supplies to see them through
The burning days, the freezing nights,

Must be secured inside: leaf and stem
Incorporate. And bright flowers springing
From cactus tips like Athene fully-armed
From the head of Zeus, will flare so furiously,

They'll burn out within a single day or night.

The Maquis Landscape

Dalmatia to Greece

Two flowerings.

One of moisture,
One of drought;
One of rainbows,
One of heat and light.

One of Spring:
Green hillsides,
Flowering meadows.
One of Summer:
Pricking needles,
Thorny thickets,
Ripening berries.

One of youth:
Fresh hopes
And promise.
One of age:
The heat turned up,
Hillsides parched,
The flowers withered.

Two flowerings.

The second out of
Heat and drought:
Aromatic oils,
Perfumes, fruits:
Sun's quintessence,
Substance
Of heat and light.

Tree of Life

Start at The Crown in Paradise.
It overlooks a palm-fringed lake
Where white yachts tack in the breeze
And people at their ease lie stretched
On balconies basking in the glitter
Of the rocking waves, Sun's ceaseless

Scattering of jewels. Then face about
To the Mountain. Gain the dappled shade
Of the broad-leaved woods, carpets
Of wood anemones, the quiet shuffle
At your feet of last year's leaves.

Mounting, you'll enter darker greens,
Deeper shade. Broad leaves shrink
To needle-points, blossoms to woody cones.
No shuffle underfoot. The softness
Of shed needles compounds the silence
Of your tread. You climb on through

Mute stillness of the evergreens,
Glimpse through breaks in the trees
Paradise far below, The Crown shining
In its grove of palms, the jewel
That is the lake. The Mountain
You're scaling is the Tree of Life.

Its roots lie deep in the snows
And rocks above. Beyond the limits
Of the forest, steep hillsides open

Onto flowering meadows of gentians,
Harebells, whites and golds
Of ox-eye daisies, orchids, pimpernels.

And so, your continuing ascent
Transforms into a kind of homecoming,
A return to roots that baffle thought.
Giddy drops unsettle your balance,
Gigantic rocky faces overwhelm
As if willing you to shrink, contract,

Prostrate yourself like the clinging mats
Of alpines already lost to the high
Pastures left behind; stems, leaves
Drawn ever tighter like coiled springs
Compressed into the root. Within
The climb of these few hours you've

Worked a vertical passage to the poles,
To the bare lives of lichen clamped
On rock; and Time itself's wound back
To its beginnings when dumb rocky faces
Such as these were themselves alive
(Or so your sense of kinship claims)

And now root-like, root-hardened, still
Rear indispensable to life, from the lichens
To the meadows and forests reaching
To the lake and those taking their ease
Among the palms of Paradise. Listen!
The sole sounds you'll hear among

The roots of the Tree of Life

    are the trickles of melting ice.

Algae

The seaweeds

Plant phantoms disgorged at low tide,
Stranded on the sand or draped over rocks
And helpless to support themselves;

Floated later or left salt-encrusted,
To stiffen, the Sea's harvest
Of arrested waves, nutrient-rich;

Flowerless, fruitless, swaying
To the movement of wind on wave,
The drag and surge of tides. The World's

Dream Time; life before dry land, shaped
By water in worlds of make-believe,
Deadman's fingers, mermaid's hair, strings

Of streaming ribbons, branching tongues,
Brown, red, olive-green; sea meadows
Of moss-like forms, and forests of holdfasts,

The leaf-stems climbing through the cool
Blue-green veil towards the lit surface,
There to harness a World's future

Out of the Sun's transforming rays.

Mosses

The green world creeps ashore.

Lowly first steps
Beyond the Sea's womb-like bouyancy
Spread a surface softness over the drying land.

Plantlets, each individual,
Not yet able to stand rooted and alone
But grouped together, compact, low-growing,

Cushion the emerging ground,
Moulding the hardening edges of the rocks
Into Fairyland, a World through the Looking Glass.

Each infant stem
Thin as a spider's thread with leaves
Minutely toothed or feathery, plumed or curled

Almost into rings:
Forms as precise and varied
As the flowering Earth to come; the early World

Dressed in Moss,
Transforming into soil below,
The sunlit alchemy of its fine-wrought leaves

Raising the air above.
Even its tiny *Pixie Hoods*, spore-
Capsules hoisted on thread-like stems,

Are vestiges
Of a World seeking ways of growing up.

Lichen

More mineral than plant?
Yet outlasting their weathering substrates:
Propagation for them a form
Of flaking, crumbling.

These flat white patches
On our garden steps will outlive me,
As will the grey-green powder
Crumbling on the garden wall;

Cratered surfaces of tiny scales,
They erupt with stalks, balancing
Minute cups coated with finest
Powdery fruit of spores:

Fungi weaving a network
That anchors and protects, Algae
Using sunlight cookery for both.
First steps in symbiosis.

A World of crusts and scales,
Flat patches, leaf-like lobes, powdery
Or jelly-like, rough warty surfaces;
And thriving,

More fully embodied,
In the clearer air of the hills:
Dangling from gnarled hawthorn trees,
Feeding on sunlight and thin air;

Tufts of hair-like branches, matted
Or wispy like teased wool, or antler-forked.
And living on in highest
Mountain reaches,

Or beyond the range
Of moss in tundra contracted flat
As a surface mark, seemingly
More embedded in the rock:

A living memorial
To what's embraced in life's extremes
And the enduring union of opposites.
And etched as Nature's

Ineffaceable tattoos, all over
Our gravestones and memorials.

Fern

Is Janus-like;
Facing forwards,
Looking back:

A mound of coiled tongues,
Fronds in a sunward arc

Declining, earth-bound

To spore-specks like those
Of Fungi- facing down;

*

Its life-cycle leaps
Between disjointed halves

As though plant and beast
Were still conjoined

Or Fern forests not yet
Turned to coal, while

Algal scales smaller
Than your little fingernail

Surface on the air to uncurl
Fern's forward-facing magic:

The earth beneath, the elements,
Sunlight above, composed

Into the countless variations
Of the leaf.

Mushrooms

Rise from underground overnight,
Sunshields in place. Strange white blooms
Studding the grass, a veil attaching stalk
To fruiting cap as if infants scarcely
Out of the cot. No leaf or shoot

And teetering helplessly without
The mothering mesh of filaments below
Predigesting the nourishment that's
Pushed them up-aloft. And for what?
Lacking roots, they've no means

Of springing back once trampled
Or knocked flat. But that's no matter.
They're fruits of Earth not Sun.
Flowers of metabolism, their dust
Of a million spores earthbound

On a mission to prise apart
What needs breaking down.

Fungi

Earth's year-round Hallowe'en.
Lunar reflections of the flowering plant
That repel and fascinate: fleshy
Body-parts, jelly-like ears
That appear on rotting logs,

Or racks of bracket fungi
Pursed like grossly protruding lips
Or the fabled Fly Agaric: all-clear
Spots of white on red for danger,

And names that speak for themselves:
  Death Cap, Destroying Angel.

Or what's first announced by stench:
Stinkhorn's *witch's eggs* hoisting
Its flowering stem with slug and fly-
Attracting slime, stinking parody

Of fragrant blossom, of bee
And butterfly. A world apart
From the circulating breeze,
Breath of sunlight, stalk and leaf.

Earth's emerging underground
Of pallid flesh, of flaccid gills
And putrid smells whose sole
Determined task in growing,
Fruiting is to digest, digest.

Return remains to fertile dust.

Parasitic Fungi

Blame the wet, the warmth, the weather?
Spots of spores, dust specks, become
Cancerous cells, exuberant forces
Of disintegration but in the wrong place;

Breaking bounds, a law unto themselves:
Downy, powdery mildews, moulds, blights
And wilts, scabs and rusts, prising open
Unlawful entry into living tissue.

Or Honey Fungus extracting its own
Living from its lethal penetration
Of root and trunk; shade and airy crown
Annulled, patterned bark, distinctive grain.

Blame the weather for rampant Earth-cells?
Networks of white rot broken loose
Of cosmic ordering? Whence unlawful
Freedom? Trespass? Shining Lucifer's

Fatal spot of taint?

Seed Knowledge

Seed Knowledge

Roots before shoots; whether
Palest threads of bulbs, delving
Tap roots, snaking rhizomes,
Fine-branched networks; and

How best to harvest water,
Vital salts to serve the trials
Of light, mounting up-aloft
And out of sight. All's vigour

Below ground in growing tip,
The finest fragile hair. Every seed
Knows it's roots first: touchdown.
Immersion in the Earth Mother.

Branching out in the dark.

A World Apart

Roots. A World apart. Knowing no 'Up-above'.
Blind to That which they sustain. So Seed-
Rumours of a World beyond the range
Of rooting eyes, are met with scorn. A World

Of light? Look about you. All's damp and dark.
'But,' pipe up the Rootlets 'What of the Great
Plant Being the Seeds speak of? They say we're
Such a vital part.' Their woody Elders, in reply:

'The legends of our Dream Time? Those fables
Of Stem and Leaf, of Bud and Blossom beneath
A warming Sun? Charming. But our most
Far-seeing Roots throughout all generations

Have searched the furthest reaches of the dark
And discovered not the slightest trace. Rootlings:
Believe us, Seeds sow mischief. There's only
The dark, these myriad minerals we're to harvest –

Who knows why – and why should we ever need to ask?
Rest content with work and wondering at the dark.'

Stem and Leaf

Dark and night, day and light.
Breathing in, breathing out.

Now contracting into stem,
Now expanding into leaf,

Provisions for the mission
Gathered daily and for free.

Jacob's ladder night and day,
Manifest from ditch to field;

Earth ascending, light
Descending: transformed

To manna in the leaf.

Bud

Leaf steps
At rhythmic intervals
Mount the spindly tower
Of the stem, quickening

Towards the growing point
For Light's descent
In the swaying air.
A secret Summit there,

A new intensity at work
In the closed sphere
Of the tight-packed bud.
What will unfold

Will be a wonder to behold.

Pollen Specks, Nectar Sips

Plants are fragments
Of the rainbow,
The elements taken root,
Held fast by a spell of earth.

To bud, to blossom
Is their release
Let colour, fragrances
Stream upon the breeze,

Call into motion a world
Winged as they can never be,
Drone and buzz and hum,
Tireless activity

Of fly and bee sparking to life
The season's nourishment,
The future's seed, with
Dusty pollen specks

And tiny nectar sips.

Pollen Hoard

The Rainbow's sprung roots;
Its colours conceived
In rhythmic motion
Between earth and sky.

Blossoms beckon,
Petal-wings to left and right,
Keels horizontal
For a firm landing.

Bee enters, explores inside,
Is offered nectar, withdraws
Coated in dust of the pollen hoard;
Rainbow's rumoured

Pot of gold finally yielded up.

Cuttings

The Tree of Life in every stem;
The seven stages of growth
Potential in each eye or node.

Cut off and earthed, the vigour
Remains, the part still held within
The mothering force. Cuttings

Remind us: to be cut off means
Either to wither, be cast away,
Or earthed, to root, shoot, come

To leaf and bud, to flower and fruit.
It all depends on being returned
To earth. That, and the choice

Of Gardener.

Trees

Raised-up soil.

The Earth's a spring
Meandering through
The green world of plants

Welling to a river network
In every tree, each trunk

Of lifeless bark a life-
Forged signature,

Oak, Ash, Birch...
Heart wood also, cast off

As once the minerals;
Rocks crumbling to soil

Raised up once more
On the life-stream,

Earth's Dream which
Grants to every tree

Its crown.

Celebrations

Ivy

Flourishes in deep shade. Bursts
Into the spring light, holding up
Leaves like shields freshly forged
For the advance. Fibrous roots
Along each stem clamp in place
As up it snakes, decking out
The chosen host after its own
Fashion. Stems dangle or adhere
To branches, secure enough
For flowerheads to flourish
Among the clustered overgrowth
Each opened blossom a harbinger
Of the black-ribbed fruits to come.

'Parasite', we declare, and set
To work sawing, lopping, chopping.
Ropes of it thick enough to haul
The old horse barges, or strings
Of it to pull and pull until you feel
You're unravelling the hedge:
All leaves and stem; no need
Of a trunk when others oblige
Winding its upward way as if,
Like them, aspiring to a crown.
But no parasite. Just out of place:
All the vigour of the ancient woodland
Tumbling into your domestic space.

*

Ever green. Food and shelter
At the threshold of winter:

Insects sip its nectar before
The long sleep, birds build up

Their stores of fat from the late
Black fruits. Woven into wreaths

In ancient Greece to honour
An athlete's victory,

Or newly-weds entwined
In faithful love, poets too

For their winning verses: ivy
Arrived at its elusive crown

By way of our esteem,
Deemed fit for honouring

Fruits of our humanity;
The next moment we're

Pulling at it, lopping, chopping,
Tearing it down.

Garlic Mustard

Spring arising in ranks along the verges
So tall and straight; large sunny green leaves
Heart-shaped, wavy edges. They mount
The spindly stems at steep-stepped intervals
Contracting as the summit nears
And the clustering buds blossom:

Flowers you'd not expect from so tall
A stalk and such board-leafed promise.
Is this all the magic Jack-by-the Hedge
Can conjour? This hedgerow cap
Of tiny crucifers; so many full-stops
As though enough's enough? While

The Stem shoots on regardless,
Marshalling the flowers into spike-like pods
As spindly as itself, long fingers
Skywards-stretching, seeds by the score
Preparing for release... But – only pluck
A leaf and taste: *Poor Man's Mustard!*

Europe's oldest spice, savour stored
In every part; garlic oil in a wild cabbage
Unknown to the Garlic family.
Jack's magic mustard hard at work,
Neither time nor need for blossoming
Extravagance. And see – how well

The cap fits. Should hoverflies
Not do their work, Garlic Mustard
    Will self-fertilise.

Creeping Buttercup

Lustrous petals, so smooth
On the inside they reflect the light:
Sungold brimming over meadow,
Hedgerow, roadside verge;

Lawns as well, as they're indifferent
To mowers slicing them to shreds.
Within days they're back, sungazing,
Their mazy network undisturbed.

They reach high as the meadow grasses
Or low as your lawn requires and have
Nothing to do with cures for lunacy
Or the colour of butter; rather,

The leap from leaf to bud: leaves,
Splayed like a crow's foot, diminishing
As they mount the stem, shrinking
Into single tiny blades as though

There's nothing more for a leaf to do
But disappear, make way for something
Utterly new, arriving veiled in secrecy
And emerging Sun-warmed, fully formed

Out of the blue.

The Brassicas

A Celebration from Turnip to Rapeseed

Turnip

First, the flags of green
Then the round white hull

Of the submarine breaking air,
Bouyed up for all to see: a root

Arisen, stable anchorage achieved.

Cabbage

The bud swells
As if magnified
By some monstrous lens
Or fierce cataract of force
Directed to this end.

What of the flower?

Put on hold, forgotten
In the cascade
Of leaves infolding:
Giant ears deaf
To anything but

Their part in growing
A cabbage head
And a cabbage heart.

*

Or buds sprouting from
Leaf axils hugging the stem,
Repeat in a myriad

Miniature cascades,
Cabbage's unwitting feat:
Brussel Sprouts, best left

Until the judicious touch
Of frost releases them
To be (for some) their special

Christmas dinner treat.

*

Or should the Stem itself respond,
Plump its own pale flesh
Into a squat globe, hoisting
Leafy stalks from top and sides:

Kohlrabi: swelling with titles:
Grand Duke, White Vienna,
Purple Danube... but really,
Wild Cabbage, boundless

Vitality in yet another guise
Waltzing into the kitchen
Offering the savour of
Its mild turnip flavour

Complete with tender crunch.

*

Or should leaf remain leaf, not
Driven into the vortex of the bud,

Compelled to undergo the perils
Of hard-heading, (or heartening up)

But leafing on, curly-thick, water's
Green embodiment, wave after wave

Rising in the wash of the midrib,
A living sea of minerals, vitamins:

Kale's hardy nourishment,
(Even in the face of cruellest frosts.)

*

Yet more:

We urge Cabbage on
Skywards, beyond leaf,
Stem, bud, raise it into

The upright, a waist-high
Edible tree, a forest canopy
Of tight-clustered florets

On massy trunks of green:
A nutritional powerhouse,
Science declares of Broccoli,

Flowering crest of the wild
Cabbage wave.

*

Finally:

A Brassica left to flower,
Burns in the bright sun
To a dazzling yellow glare.

Brilliant acres light up
Among our sober fields
As though some alien

Had stolen in undercover
Of watery green and now:
Discarded its disguise,

Broken loose, burst
Into flame its pollen-fume
Itching our eyes as it

Disperses on the breeze,
Leaving in its wake
Swelling pods, blackening seeds.

Brassica, its sun-warmed
Summit attained; from turnip
Submarine breaking the surface

Of the soil to sun-blessed,
Cold-pressed, health-enhancing
Rapeseed cooking oil.

Onion

Bedded in earth as the Earth-globe
In its field of stars. Plumped
To squat on the surface
Held by rudimentary threads.

Peel back the tunicated leaves,
The papery brown membrane,
Its longitudinal lines tapering
To meet above, below; progress
Layer by layer through green
To white, each with its own
Fine, slimy film, each tunic
Enfolding another: a cosmic
Earth laboratory busy throughout
The growing season cooking all
That the warmth-laden force fields
Of light, air, moisture can provide.

So Onion blooms under wraps,
Locked down. Eyewatering:
Essence of mustard oils when diced
And put in the pot; sizzling
Foundation for savoury tastes.

Left to seed, Onion's tiny flowers
Are of no significance compared
With the spherical inflorescence
Of which they're part: as below,
So above, the globe repeated
On a stalk, indifferent to Earth's
Gravity, the cardinal directions.

Onion: still with its head in the clouds;
Not quite touched down. A sphere.
An Onion-Cosmos, quietly
        Resting in itself.

Stinging Nettle

Wake up! In a flash
Your hand's withdrawn
Too late. It's brushed
A leaf and brittle spikes
Have lodged a burning
Acid under your skin.

Wake up! Nettles have
No use for sweet-smelling
Flourishes of flowers.
Stem and leaves bristle
With hairs primed
To strike fire, needle-sharp.

Amidst the sleeping
Innocence of greenery,
Nettle's stirring
In its sleep, that burning
Prick to your hand,
Its dream of awakening.

*

Paired leaves ordered in tier
Upon tier, four-square, all
Directions covered. Leaf margins
Strongly serrated, bristling
As in militant self-defense
And uninhibited, constantly
On the move underground,
Fresh recruits springing from nodes
Of snaking yellow rhizomes.

They muster in patches
Where the manure was dumped
Or under trees where animals
Have been in search of shade,
Or following in our footsteps,
Massed in forgotten corners,
Or neglected compost heaps,
And always signalling fertility,
Their vigour a stimulus to growth
Or the ferment of decomposition.

Their blossoms are so many afterthoughts,
Dangling like strings of tiny beads
But never their growth's culmination
Like the fire burning in their brittle spikes
On leaves which play exclusive host
To munching black caterpillars.

Stinging Nettle: a crucible for life
To reach beyond itself, birth
Plant-creatures winged and flying:
Small Tortoiseshells, Peacock
Butterflies; only – rooted Nettle

Is sleeping, unaware that dreams
Come true. No eyes to see
The mystery it's helped set free:

Those fiery-formed,
    winged blossoms.

Honeysuckle

Bare woody stems transformed
To a mass of dark green leaves
Well in advance of the dormant trees
And hedgerows. It could be

A free-standing bush were its stems
Not so tightly coiled its spiral twists
Might be left embedded in the branches
Of its hosts. And in advance also

Of Spring's bright emerald; winding
Its darkling way towards Midsummer,
Golden candelabra aflame on the evening air
As twilight fades into the warmth

Of a Summer's night. Nocturnal life
Awakens to the summons
Of its fragrance and moths flutter
Into its wide-stretched nectar depths.

A Bouquet of Herbs

The Sun's plunged to the root.
Leaf-swelling moisture has been
Offset, showy blossoms displaced
As sunlight's absorbed throughout.

Now, even names speak their fragrance:
Rosemary, Sage, Lavender, Thyme..
Undergrowth of twisting stems
Stiffening to wood and flaking bark;

Earth's mineral force arising to tangle
With ethereal warmth in narrow slips
Of leaves; Rosemary in sombre
Needle-green, softer blue-greys

Of Lavender, tiniest Thyme creeping
Over the garden path or tumbling
From a ledge. Distilleries of light.
They refine the dialogue of Earth

And Sky, each leaf within its own
Minute compass secreting
Fragrance of essential oils: drops
Of liquid blossom, Earth's fiery dew.

A Bouquet
of Dead Nettles

White, Red, Yellow Archangel

Leaves paired also, but no
Bristling appearence,
Toothed edges rounded,
Leaf surfaces downy soft
And flowers bunched about stems
Like gaily-coloured ruffs:

No shrinking signs of deference
To the liquid blossoms
Of essential oils nor brittle
Acid stings; their own have been
Outsourced to bumbling Bees
Drawn to snuggle between

Their blossoms' flaring lips,
Wide-set as if in tireless
Proclamation of an offered
Entrance into Bliss:
Its nectar sips, its stamens
Of black and gold lying

Side by side in innocent
Oblivion. Square-set
Sheltering towers; Archangels
White, Yellow, Red,
Spreading protective shade
Over *Adam-and-Eve-in-the-Bower.*

Orchid

Eye-catching. Roots glinting
Up-aloft in the humid air,
Absorbing moisture without need
Of the mundane earth. Strange

Blossom-faces, organ-like shapes
Of insect-animals, lips and tongues
In colourful cascades averted
From the sun's gaze beneath
The filtering forest canopy

And turned to a world of wings,
Humming creatures
Intimately adapted to serve
Their one and only need:

To flower, flower...
      dreams

Suspended in the air, reaching
Into realms of fantastical extravagance
And all-consuming,
No residual force to spare that's fit
For nourishment or healing.

They're still earth-averse
In our Northern latitudes, seeds
Lingering in germinal suspense
Until kissed awake by some
Mothering mycorrihza from
The sunken sunless underworld.

It's thanks to Fungi gorgeous Orchid
May enter into life, grace
Our meadows with its flowers.

Dandelion

Lodges in the finest cracks. Delves
Deep raising mineral sustenance
Inaccessible to shallower roots.
But who cares? Those up-welling
Saw-toothed leaves exasperate
The tidy mind which knows
What follows from the root's tip
That weeding leaves behind:

Dandelion returns, returns.
Ineradicable its blind urge
Towards the light. Leaves
Spring up without even needing
A stem. And then- it's straight
Into the fan-vaulting; a central
Milky-hollow flower stalk
Raising a floral chapter house

For floret rays to assemble
Within the community
Of The Golden Flower-Head
In which they all combine,
In the open air, beneath a roof
Of sky, for Sun-worship,
(Closing at night). But that's
Not all. This worship bears

Its fruit as the florets wilt,
Are pushed aside by hair-like
Parachutes, each bearing its seed,
The golden disc remodelled
Downy-soft and grey, rounded
Into a sphere. The dandelion clock
Ticks down, Sun worship soon
To be transformed into air-borne flight.

Daisy

Bellis Perennis

Day's Eye

Opening with the dew
Then trodden underfoot,
Too common-small
To be taken notice of;
Or sheared clear in mowing
For the lawn's required
Restful blank of green.

Yet once collected
By the sackful for juicing
And soaking bandages
To bind the Legions' wounds
And the one *blissful sight* that
Could soften all Chaucer's sorrow.

Oh, flower of new beginnings!
Ups-a-daisy: the ready arm
To steady us, set us back on our feet.

White florets, each raying out
Its pure praise from the collective
Heart of gold. More than
A nymph with a pretty face,
Daisy-chains of childhood;

The flowering World come
Of age, ray and disc combined,
Flowers within the one Flower,
Self-surpassing. Tiny suns
Broadcasting light,
Scattered among the grass.

Lily

Flower of the Annunciation

A scaly bulb shut tight
Against all weathers:
No sight of earth.

Paradise sealed in an ark
Packed with provisions
For journeying and ready
For landfall.

As the Sun blinks through mist,
Lily stretches a stem,
Exchanges leaves for petals

And raises her white trumpet
As a rainbow frames the world
With promise:

Fanfare of warmth and light
Sunflare of streaming fragrance;
Angelic visitation?

Your nose inhales
but the words fail.

Afterwords

Blue and Gold

Here in the shadow of light
Under the leafing honeysuckle,
A blue bench. And a small
Rock garden flooding with green
In a Spring tide of *Windflowers*
Spreading across stone
And gravel surfaces; dormant life
Re-entering time, drawn from
Darkness into the sphere
Of sunlit air and hoisting frail
Flower stalks like standards
Signalling their advance.
White petals for peace, bare
Boundaries overrun, realms
Of plant and mineral merging
Yet quite distinct each gracing
The other innocent, oblivious.

Renewed beginnings with no end
But to grow onward, spreading
In all directions and ever
Surpassing lowly origins:
For the flat leaf infolds, swells
To bud, transforms to worlds
Within, without, outpouring
Blossom, fragrance, colour;
Calls into being of necessity
Creatures root-free, winged
And bound to seek out nectar,
Pollen, the quintessential.

So why should it be any
Different for me, awake
To read this Paradise-dream,
Sitting on this blue bench
Under the leafing honeysuckle,
In the shadow of light

Beneath a sky of blue and gold?

Gaining Ground?

Earth, a seed long buried
In winter ground,
The rocks at once its husk
And weathered soil,

Cast-offs themselves;
Residues of Epochs
Confounding thought;

Life self-consumed
Like the phoenix
Whose ashes compose
The ground of its future arising.

Earth, a seed in chaos
Of breaking down;
Wildernesses taking hold

Or the roots of our humanity
Gaining ground?

Evolution

The World's at war with itself.
Nature too, mirrors back our state of being.
Earthquake, fire and flood
Bury, burn and drown,
While out of the air high explosives
Tumble defenceless cities to the ground.

How precious, then, the truths
This garden-bible of ours unfolds!
These ferns, unsheathed
To their fullest reach,
Cross curved blades in a green peace;
In the World's long life, their leafy

Inflorescence has never progressed
To flower and seed. Yet the World's moved on
From the silent tongues
Of unfurling fronds,
Evolved in such a way (and before
Our blood-soaked battlefields) that plants

Could progress beyond root
And leaf, beyond green upon green,
To the fullness
Of the sun-fed flower,
Its scent and colour, fruit and seed:
Could evolve for Earth in such plain sight

The riches of the gifts of light.

Raking Leaves

It's the mellow light of evening calls me out
Raking leaves mixed up in the hosta patch
Under the magnolia tree; combing
The flaccid yellowing stems, drooping
Or pulped flat, till they pull clear and join
The leaves retrieved for composting.

The gravel spread there to deter slugs
And snails is once again laid bare.
Close by a flurry of wings signals
Robin's prompt arrival to enquire,
Explore the opened spaces newly raked.
Framed through the branches of the tree

The sky's still blue with white dustings
Of clouds. Distant sounds carry on the silence;
The sleepless drone of engines, sheep
In the fields. Raking leaves admits
Of Autumn's stepchange, its approaching
Cliff-edge to nowhere. For us, the melting

Glow of golden light, the holy calm,
Presages cold, discomfort, lengthening dark.
For Earth, it's the lingering end of dreaming:
Winter its wake-up call to let slip
Material sheaths, holiday in spaceless Sun,
From which all rooted life re-emerges

Refreshed, renewed, re-formed.

And Finally

Mistletoe

Berries like dull pearls, touched down
As bird-shit or stropped onto a bough
From a thrush's beak and left to germinate
Way-up in the tree tops; *rock-a-bye-baby*
Cradled in the living wood, suckers
Securely anchored from tumbling down;

Paired leaves remain as if seedlings
Wide-spread in perpetual flight.
They branch in perfect dichotomy,
Dangle like ragged nests or hives,
Or round out over years into airy spheres
Following the cycle of their unearthly life

Indifferent to sun and earth: nectar
In winter, winter fruit to follow. Cosmic
Enclaves from another past never
To fall into the full-fledged ways of Earth;
Too young (so the Norse myth goes)
To be asked to take the Oath to do

No harm, and seized upon by the Evil One
As the one wounding point whose very
Other-worldliness brought bright Baldur low.
And so, at the time of the Christmas Birth
We resolve death's paradox: bring it home
And hang it high and think to kiss

Beneath the Mistletoe.

Glossary

Glossary

axil
the upper angle between leaf and stem or branch and trunk

corolla
a collective term for the petals of a flower

inflorescence
the process of producing flowers, blossoming; in the case of the fern, the unfurling fronds being the furtherest expression of its 'blossoming'.

mycorrhiza
fungal mycelium penetrating the roots of a plant and supplying it with nourishing material.

panicle
literally, a 'swelling', loose and irregularly spreading clusters of seedheads as with the 'flowering' grasses; (loosely) an irregular inflorescence.

pedicel
if the main stalk of a flowering plant is the 'peduncel' the pedicel is the part of the stalk immediately bearing the flower, or the subordinate stalks each bearing a flower in a branching inflorescence.

rosette
a close-radiating group of leaves, usually pressed close to the ground.

salver

from the Sp. *salva,* the precautionary tasting of the monarch's food as presented on a plate or tray, hence *salvar,* to save. Botanically: refers to a corolla with a long tube finishing in spread-out petals.

spathe

a sheathing-leaf enclosing the inflorescence of certain plants before their expansion.

thrum and pin

primroses have two slightly different types of flowers. In 'pin-eyed' flowers the stigma is at the top of the flower tube and appears like a small green pin head. The anthers are half way down the tube ringing the style. In the 'thrum-eyed' kind the opposite applies so the stigma is half way down the tube while the anthers are at the top, appearing as a yellow-orange mass.

tubercle

a small tuber

umbel

flat-topped inflorescence in which the flower stalks all spring from the same point at the top of the stalk. Think umbrella!

whorl

leaves, flowers or parts of the flower springing from the stem or axis at the same level and encircling it.

By the same author published by Wynstones Press:

Poems for Younger Children

During his years of teaching within the Hereford Steiner Academy, David Donaldson composed a wide variety of verses for the children of his class.

Most of the enclosed poems were originally written for particular children, but we hope this book will allow these verses to bring joy and inspiration to many more children and adults alike.

46 pages.
ISBN 9780 946206 650

Promises - A book of Poems

This second volume by David Donaldson contains a further varied collection of poems, composed during his years of teaching within the Steiner Academy Hereford. All of these verses were originally written for particular children, with inspiration from the wonderfully diverse subjects which the Steiner-Waldorf curriculum contains. We hope this book will help to bring joy to many more children and adults alike.

64 pages.
ISBN 9780 946206 308

A Treasury of Trees

Trees express the life of the Earth in all its variety, fruitfulness and mystery, from ancient beginnings to our present time. These 56 poems reflect the author's life-long love of trees; they are verses of celebration, remembrance and questioning reflection, drawing on first-hand observation and experience as well as historical research and well-known folk traditions and mythology.

A Treasury of Trees is a rich and imaginative exploration of our relationship to the Earth and all we stand to gain by entering more deeply into its life.

> *"This tree hymnal is indeed a work of devotion in which David Donaldson sings, it seems, almost every tree in Christendom, but often doing so, too, with a pagan magic."*
> Matthew Barton, New View, Autumn 2018

78 pages.
ISBN 9780 946206 810

Wynstones Press
publishes and distributes a range of
Books, Advent Calendars, Cards and Prints.
For further information please see:

www.wynstonespress.com
info@wynstonespress.com